Searchlight
BOOKS™

What's Cool
about Science?

Discover

Cutting-Edge
Medicine

Meg Marquardt

Lerner Publications ◆ Minneapolis

Copyright © 2017 by Lerner Publishing Group, Inc.

Content Consultant: Paula Deming, PhD, MT, Associate Professor of Medical Laboratory and Radiation Sciences, The University of Vermont

Lerner Publications Company
A division of Lerner Publishing Group, Inc.
241 First Avenue North
Minneapolis, MN 55401 USA

For reading levels and more information, look up this title at www.lernerbooks.com.

Library of Congress Cataloging-in-Publication Data

The Cataloging-in-Publication Data for *Discover Cutting-Edge Medicine* is on file at the Library of Congress.

ISBN 978-1-5124-0808-9 (lib. bdg.)
ISBN 978-1-5124-1285-7 (pbk.)
ISBN 978-1-5124-1064-8 (EB pdf)

Manufactured in the United States of America
1 – VP – 7/15/16

Contents

Chapter 1

WHAT IS MEDICINE?

Medicine is a science dedicated to making people healthy. Today's doctors use cutting-edge technology to do this. Some repair parts of the body. Others cure diseases. All are helping people live better, longer lives.

Today's hospitals are filled with advanced technology. What is one way that doctors keep people healthy?

The history of medicine goes back thousands of years. Ancient Greeks discovered natural treatments. For example, they used ginger to treat nausea. Ancient doctors wrote huge books full of such treatments. One of the most famous was the Arab physician Avicenna, who was born around 980 CE. His cures were used for hundreds of years.

Avicenna wrote a medical textbook called *The Canon of Medicine*. It was used by doctors into the 1600s.

Today's medicine is much more advanced. Computers help doctors diagnose diseases. Robots assist surgeons with delicate operations. Doctors use their knowledge and skills to help patients around the world.

Computers of all kinds are important parts of cutting-edge medicine.

Surgery Robots

The Da Vinci Surgical System is one popular surgery robot. The robot's arms hold surgical tools and cameras. The surgeon sits at a computer. He or she uses hand controls to move the robot's arms. The computer's screen shows the view from the cameras.

Robots make new surgeries possible. Their arms can bend and twist more than human hands and wrists. They can make tiny, precise movements. Da Vinci robots have helped with millions of operations.

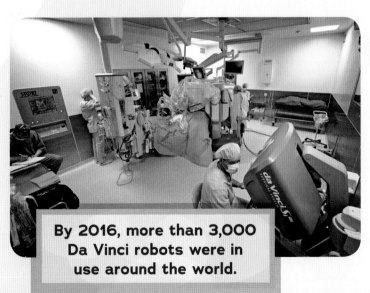

By 2016, more than 3,000 Da Vinci robots were in use around the world.

Chapter 2

ORGAN INNOVATIONS

Bodies are made up of parts called organs. The heart, the lungs, and the skin are three examples of organs. Each organ has its own job. When they work right, a person is healthy. But sometimes organs fail. This can cause serious problems.

The human heart contains powerful muscle tissue that pumps blood throughout the body. What is another example of an organ?

Transplant organs can replace failed organs. A transplant involves moving an organ from one person to another. The person who provides the organ is known as a donor.

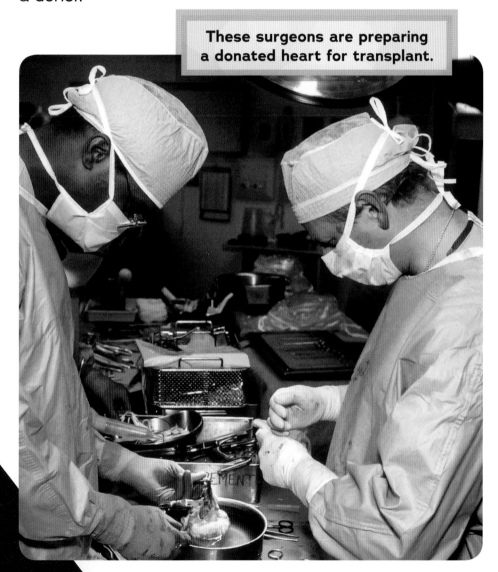

These surgeons are preparing a donated heart for transplant.

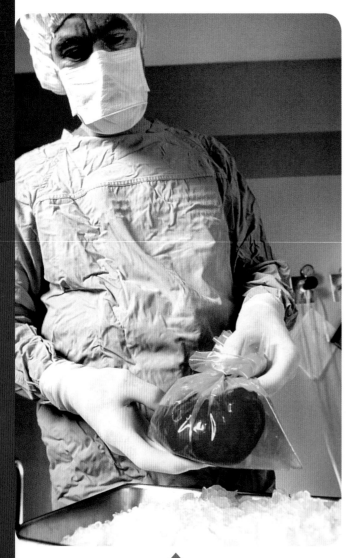

Some organs, such as kidneys, may be donated by living people. In other cases, the donor is a person who has just died. His or her organs can save a patient's life.

People can choose whether or not to be organ donors. Their choice may be marked on their driver's licenses. Doctors can quickly tell whether they are donors.

THIS DONATED KIDNEY IS READY TO BE TRANSPLANTED.

Organs are transported
in special boxes that
keep them cool.

An organ is not always available right away. It may
have to be brought from a distant hospital. Organs are
fragile. They must be kept cool and undamaged. If too
much time passes, the transplant might fail.

Cutting-edge technology is changing this. One example is a machine nicknamed the "heart in a box." It keeps donor hearts healthy until the transplant. Tubes pump blood through the heart. The heart keeps beating outside the body.

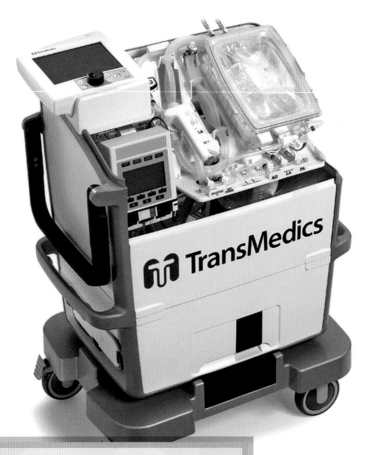

The TransMedics Organ Care System, or "heart in a box," can make transplants more effective.

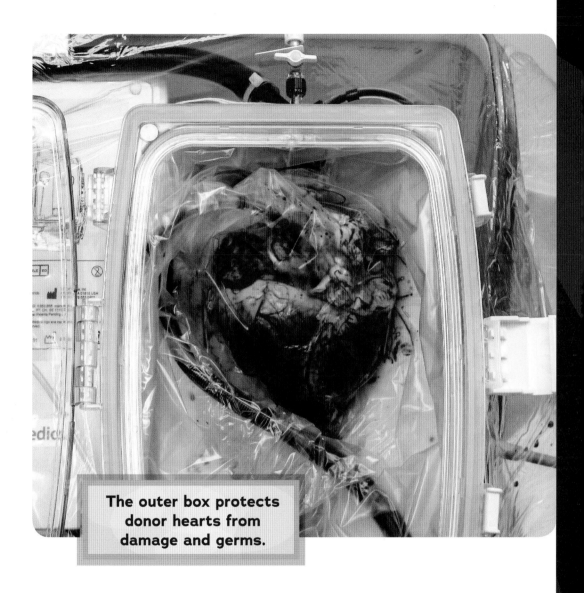

The outer box protects donor hearts from damage and germs.

The machine keeps the heart fresh for longer. Doctors have more time for the transplant. The "heart in a box" has already saved many lives.

Building New Organs

Some researchers are working on a different solution to organ failure. They are building new organs from scratch. Stem cells may make this possible.

Scientists have learned to grow some body parts, including ears, using stem cells.

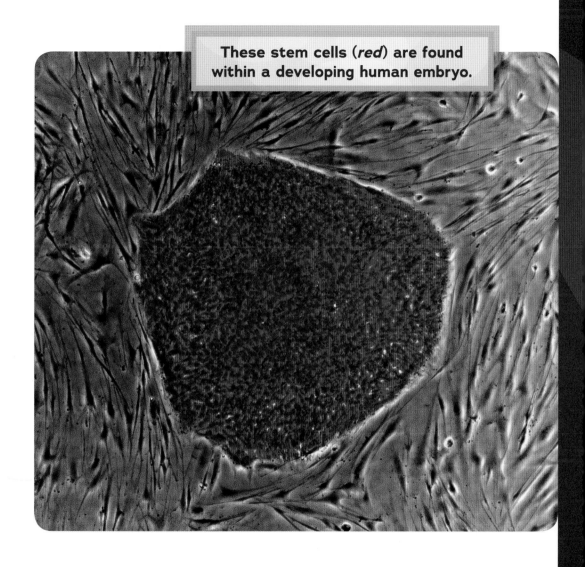

These stem cells (*red*) are found within a developing human embryo.

Cells are the building blocks of the human body. There are many different kinds of cells. Each kind of cell has its own job. But stem cells are special. They can turn into any other type of body cell. This makes them useful in building replacement organs.

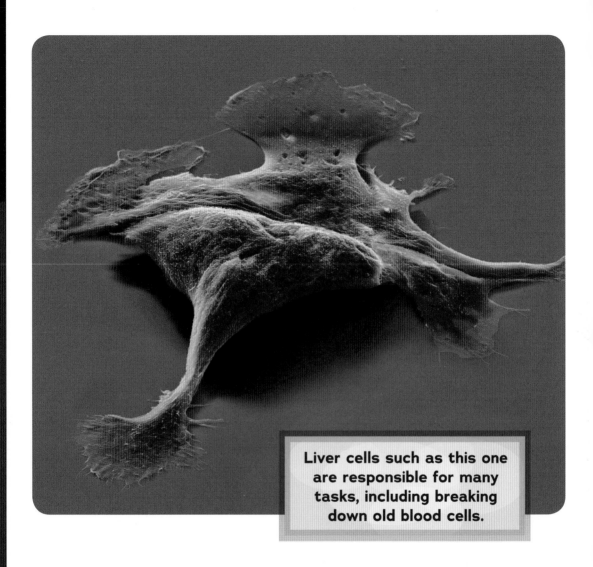

Liver cells such as this one are responsible for many tasks, including breaking down old blood cells.

Scientists have learned how to make stem cells turn into a chosen type of cell. They can even build working tissue from these cells. In 2014, scientists in Japan built small pieces of liver tissue. These mini-livers functioned in mice.

Building full-sized human organs is still a long way off. But scientists are working toward this goal. If they succeed, organ transplants will save many more lives each year.

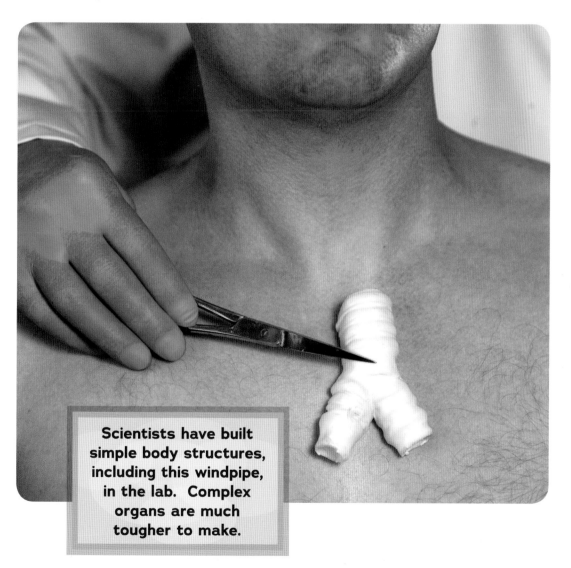

Scientists have built simple body structures, including this windpipe, in the lab. Complex organs are much tougher to make.

Chapter 3

FIGHTING DISEASE

Medicine is about more than replacing body parts. Sometimes it involves fighting illnesses. Scientists are designing new ways to combat deadly diseases.

This radiology machine is used to fight cancer. What do cancers have in common?

Battling Cancer

There are many kinds of cancer. Each kind affects different parts of the body. All kinds of cancer have some things in common. Cancerous cells all grow out of control. The cells form tumors. These tumors can spread across the body and cause many problems. If untreated, cancer can lead to death.

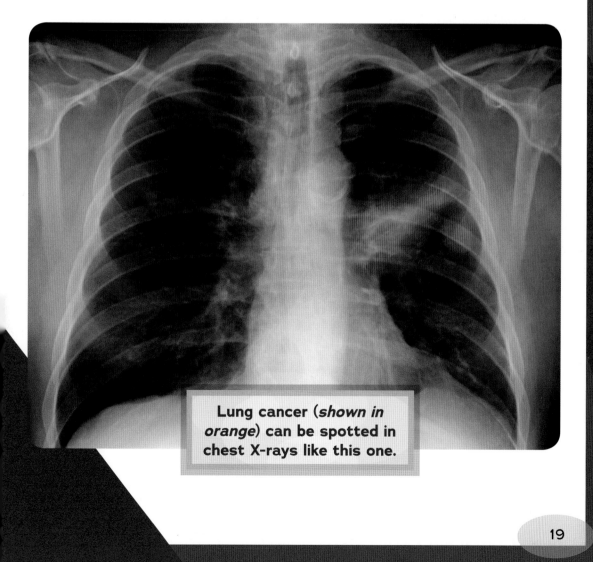

Lung cancer (*shown in orange*) can be spotted in chest X-rays like this one.

Cancer is a difficult disease to fight. Doctors try to destroy tumor cells without harming healthy cells. One possible solution is to use the body's natural defenses. The immune system usually defends against diseases. But cancer develops out of the body's own cells. The immune system may not see it as a threat.

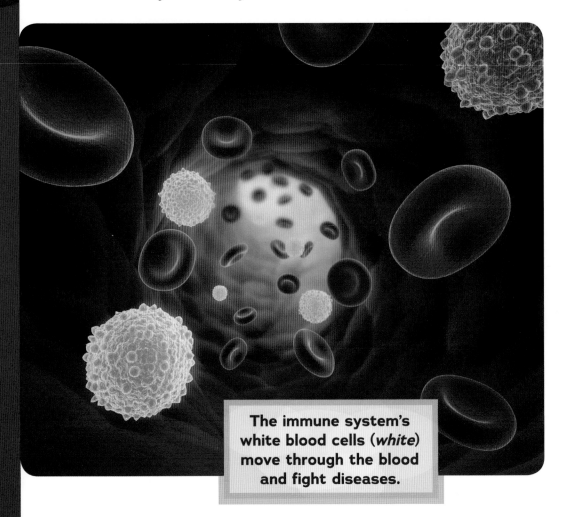

The immune system's white blood cells (*white*) move through the blood and fight diseases.

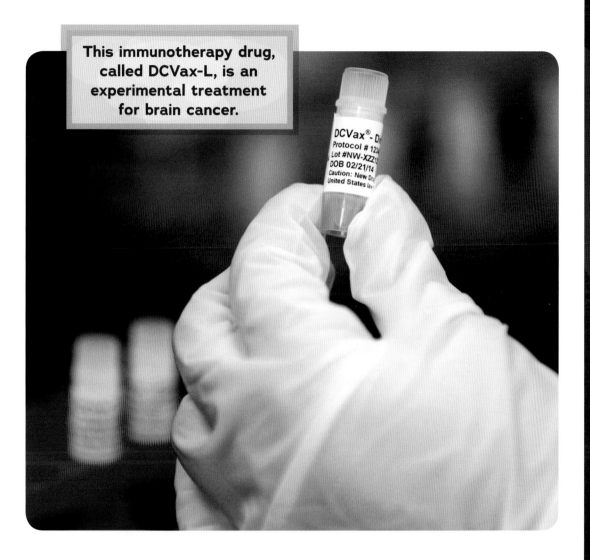

This immunotherapy drug, called DCVax-L, is an experimental treatment for brain cancer.

DCVax® - D
Protocol # 12
Lot #NW-XZZ
DOB 02/21/14
Caution: New D
United States la

Immunotherapy can change this. This procedure uses drugs that make the immune system attack the cancer. It has already been used to help fight a few types of cancer, including skin cancer and brain cancer.

Scientists are also finding ways to turn viruses against cancer. Viruses are tiny structures that cause disease. They take over cells inside the body and force the cells to create new copies of the virus. This kills the cells. Researchers are studying how viruses can target cancer cells. In the fall of 2015, the US government approved one of these treatments.

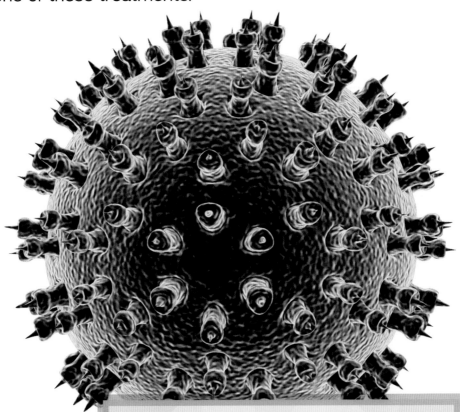

Researchers used a type of herpes virus, like the one illustrated here, to develop the treatment approved in the fall of 2015.

Sniffing Out Cancer

Scientists in Pennsylvania built a machine that senses smells. It is much more sensitive than the human nose. They are working to find out whether certain types of cancer have smells. If so, it may be possible to detect cancer earlier than ever before. The earlier a cancer is detected, the better chance the patient has of surviving.

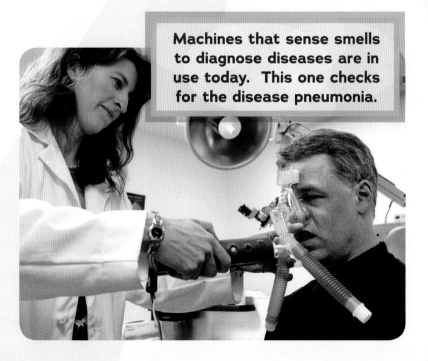

Machines that sense smells to diagnose diseases are in use today. This one checks for the disease pneumonia.

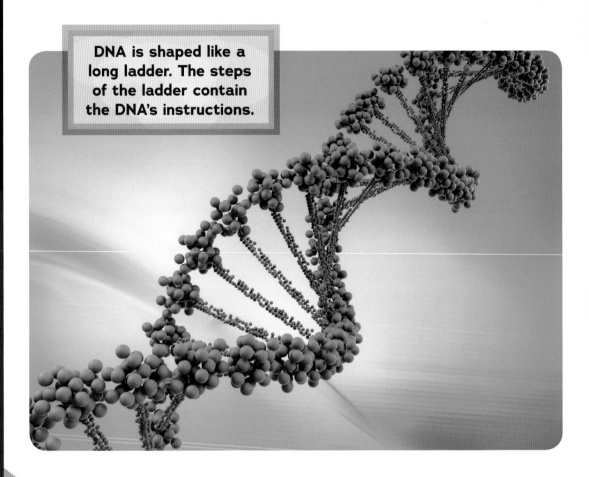

DNA is shaped like a long ladder. The steps of the ladder contain the DNA's instructions.

Gene Therapy

Almost every human cell contains a chemical called DNA. This substance is a list of instructions that makes a person unique. Hair color, eye color, and many other features are determined by DNA. Some human diseases are caused by errors within the DNA. One new disease treatment involves making changes to DNA. It is called gene therapy.

Genes are sections of DNA code. In gene therapy, scientists add or replace entire genes. For example, patients with Parkinson's disease lack a chemical called dopamine. This chemical helps them control muscle movements. A new gene therapy adds three genes that boost dopamine production. By 2014, tests of the treatment showed promising results.

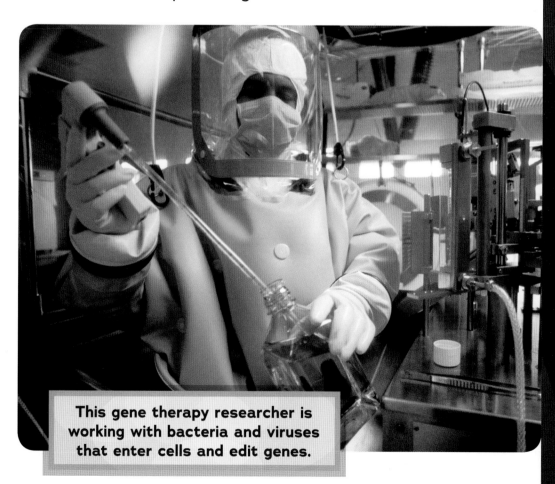

This gene therapy researcher is working with bacteria and viruses that enter cells and edit genes.

Chapter 4

MEDICAL DEVICES

Technology is changing the way medicine works in our everyday lives. Personal devices that help people stay healthy have become very popular. The simplest devices count how many steps a person takes in a day. They may look like wristbands or stopwatches. Counting steps can encourage people to exercise more.

The shrinking size of computers means they can now fit in wristband-sized devices. What can these fitness devices do?

Other devices measure heartbeats or blood oxygen levels. A user can track this information during workouts. He or she may even track it twenty-four hours a day. The data can then be viewed on a smartphone or sent to the user's doctor. It can help patients and doctors identify warning signs of disease. They can then work together to create a plan for healthy living.

SMARTPHONE APPS CAN HELP A PERSON TRACK HIS OR HER WEIGHT OVER TIME.

Ralph Lauren's smart shirt, known as PoloTech, can wirelessly send data to a smartphone or smartwatch.

1200 Cal.

The most cutting-edge health trackers are built directly into clothing. In 2015, the company Ralph Lauren introduced a smart shirt. The shirt contains sensors that track heart rate and movement. It uses this data to estimate how many calories a person burns. But this advanced technology comes at a cost. The shirt costs around $300.

A new advance in 2016 may lead to improvements in smart shirts. A team of South Korean scientists developed a thin, stretchy device around the size of a postage stamp. The device senses and stores heart-rate data. Its flexibility makes it more durable than the sensors used today.

Monitoring Diabetes

Tracking information about the body is especially important for people with diabetes. This disease prevents the body from balancing sugar levels in the blood. Diabetics use a drug called insulin to help correct these levels.

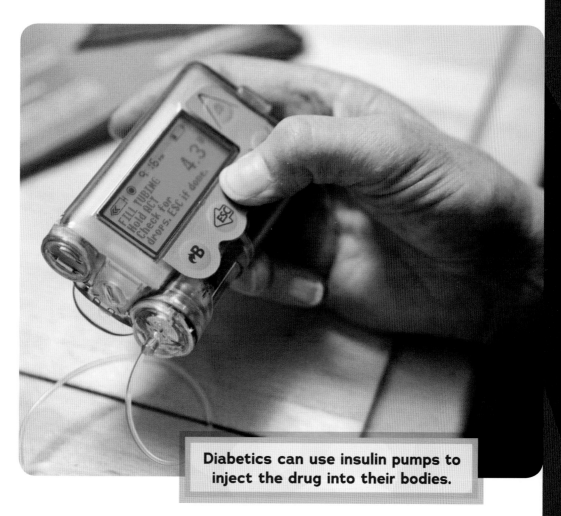

Diabetics can use insulin pumps to inject the drug into their bodies.

Throughout the day, diabetics must check their levels to know when to take insulin. For years, patients have had to prick a finger to collect blood to test. A handheld device measures the sugar levels from the blood sample.

Diabetics carefully track how their blood sugar changes over time.

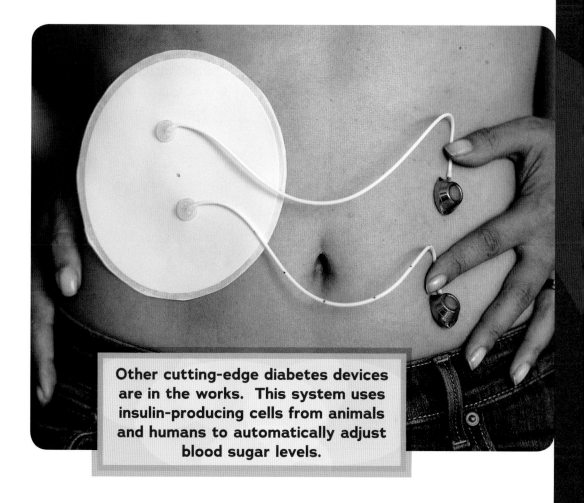

Other cutting-edge diabetes devices are in the works. This system uses insulin-producing cells from animals and humans to automatically adjust blood sugar levels.

In 2014, scientists at Princeton University developed a new testing device. It doesn't require a finger prick. Instead, it shoots light waves at the user's palm. The waves move through the skin. They are absorbed by sugar molecules in the blood. The amount of light that is absorbed tells the device how much sugar is in the blood.

On the TV show *Jeopardy!*, Watson (*center*) quickly searched through huge amounts of information to answer trivia questions.

Virtual Doctors

In 2011, a computer named Watson amazed audiences when it competed on the TV quiz show *Jeopardy!* Watson was able to quickly understand trivia questions and find the right answers. It easily beat human competitors. Doctors realized that Watson's skills might make it great at diagnosing diseases.

Watson can store and remember thousands of medical books and articles. Unlike a doctor, it can work constantly without needing food or sleep. The computer can instantly search the medical records of a patient and his or her family.

In 2011, Watson could process 500 gigabytes of information per second. That's about the same as the information in a million books.

An upgrade in 2015 allowed Watson to analyze medical images, too. By 2016, Watson was helping doctors diagnose some forms of cancer. In the future, Watson or computers like it could become a key part of any doctor visit.

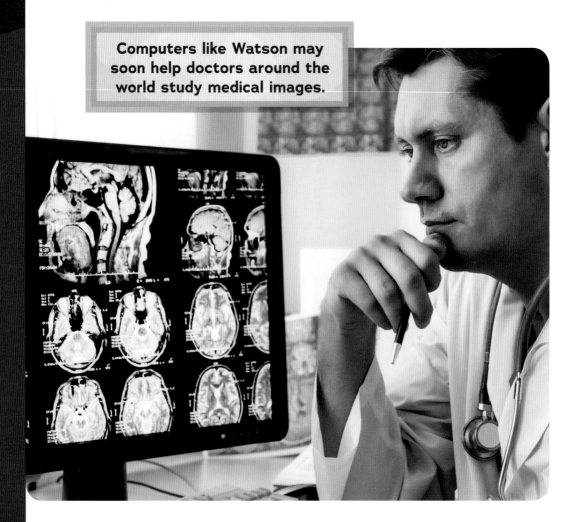

Computers like Watson may soon help doctors around the world study medical images.

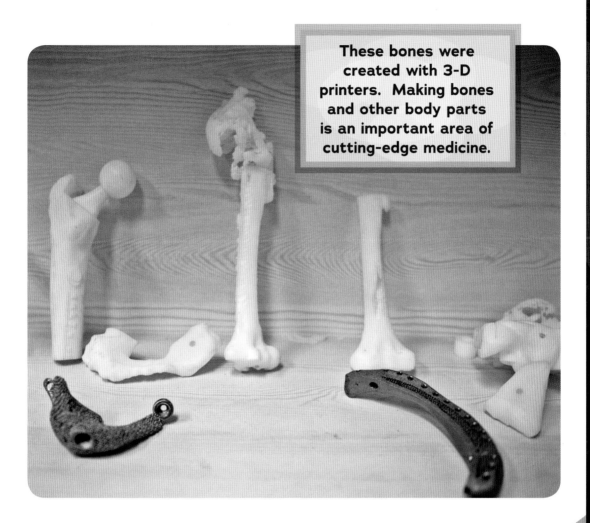

These bones were created with 3-D printers. Making bones and other body parts is an important area of cutting-edge medicine.

A Cutting-Edge Future

The future of medicine is bright. Researchers are building organs, controlling viruses, and repairing patients' genes. They are using advanced devices to track health data. They are even using computers to diagnose patients.

RESEARCHERS, DOCTORS, AND OTHER HEALTH-CARE WORKERS ARE CHANGING THE FUTURE OF MEDICINE.

▼

Cutting-edge medicine is changing the way we think about health. The work of pioneering doctors and researchers will improve patients' lives. It may even stop them from getting sick in the first place.

Smartphones and Medicine

Scientists have used smartphones to help bring medicine to remote places. One example is a portable ultrasound machine. Ultrasound machines help doctors see inside the body. This portable version attaches to a smartphone. The phone shows images from the ultrasound machine. This device could be used in small clinics that cannot afford a full-sized machine. It could also help doctors perform ultrasounds far from any medical facilities.

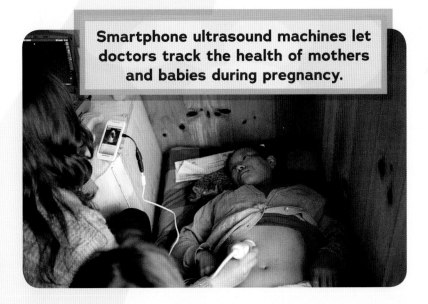

Smartphone ultrasound machines let doctors track the health of mothers and babies during pregnancy.

Glossary

cancer: a type of disease that involves out-of-control cell growth

diabetes: a disease in which the body cannot balance sugar levels in the blood

diagnose: to identify an illness or disorder

DNA: a substance that carries all genetic information in an organism

dopamine: a chemical in the brain that helps regulate body functions, including movement

gene: a part of DNA that gives rise to certain characteristics. For example, a gene determines a person's eye color.

gene therapy: adding or replacing genes to help treat a disease

immunotherapy: treating a disorder or disease by increasing the body's immune system

insulin: a substance that regulates sugar in the blood. Lack of insulin can cause diabetes.

organ: a part of the body that plays a vital role in keeping an organism alive, such as the heart or lungs

Learn More about Cutting-Edge Medicine

Books

Ballen, Karen Gunnison. *Seven Wonders of Medicine*. Minneapolis, MN: Twenty-First Century Books, 2010. Read more about seven amazing topics in cutting-edge medicine.

Bethea, Nikole Brooks. *Discover Bionics*. Minneapolis, MN: Lerner Publications, 2017. Take a look at cutting-edge breakthroughs in bionics, the science of artificial body parts.

Kenney, Karen Latchana. *What Makes Medical Technology Safer?* Minneapolis, MN: Lerner Publications, 2016. Learn how researchers and engineers are making the tools of modern medicine safe for patients.

Websites

BBC: Will We Ever Create Organs?
http://www.bbc.com/future/story/20120223-will-we-ever-create -organs
Explore the cutting-edge science of building organs in the lab.

CDC: Genetics
http://www.cdc.gov/bam/body/scoop.html
Discover more about genetics, the science behind gene therapy.

Computer History Museum: Watson
http://www.computerhistory.org/atchm/ibms-watson-jeopardy -computer-comes-to-chm
Learn more about Watson, the computer that may change the way doctors diagnose diseases.

Index

Photo Acknowledgments

The images in this book are used with the permission of: © Alexei Cruglicov/iStock.com, p. 4;
© Everett Collection/Newscom, p. 5; © Izabela Habur/iStock.com, p. 6; © Yuri Smityuk/TASS/
Newscom, p. 7; © Lightspring/Shutterstock.com, p. 8; © Doug Martin/Science Source, p. 9;
© Will & Deni McIntyre/Science Source, p. 10; © sturti/iStock.com, p. 11; © CB2/ZOB/WENN.com/
Newscom, pp. 12, 13; © Matt Dunham/AP Images, p. 14; © Scott Camazine/Science Source,
pp. 15, 19; © Eye of Science/Science Source, p. 16; © Rex Features/AP Images, p. 17; © Henrique
NDR Martins/iStock.com, p. 18; © Eraxion/iStock.com, p. 20; © Mike Brown/Reuters/Newscom,
p. 21; © RAJ CREATIONZS/Shutterstock.com, p. 22; © cosmin4000/iStock.com, p. 24; © Patrick
Landmann/Science Source, p. 25; © Joseph Kaczmarek/AP Images, p. 23; © svanhorn/iStock.com,
p. 26; © monkeybusinessimages/iStock.com, p. 27; © Brendan McDermid/Reuters/Newscom, p. 28;
© MarkHatfield/iStock.com, pp. 29, 30; © Frederick Florin/AFP/Getty Images, p. 31; © Ben Hider/
Getty Images, p. 32; © Carolyn Cole/Los Angeles Times/Getty Images, p. 33; © Andrei Malov/
iStock.com, p. 34; © ChinaFotoPress/Getty Images, p. 35; © choja/iStock.com, p. 36; © Mobisante/
Rex Features/AP Images, p. 37.

Front Cover: © Matt Dunham/AP Images.

Main body text set in Adrianna Regular 14/20.
Typeface provided by Chank.